LEMURS

by Josh Gregory

Children's Press®

An Imprint of Scholastic Inc.

Content Consultants
Dr. Stephen S. Ditchkoff and Dr. Sarah Zohdy
Professors of Wildlife Ecology and Management
Auburn University
Auburn, Alabama

Photographs ©: cover: Minden Pictures/Superstock, Inc.; 1: Andriy
Dykun/Dreamstime; 2-3 background: Genarosilva/Dreamstime; 2 lemur:
Paul Souders/Getty Images; 4, 5 background: Duncan Usher/Alamy Images; 5
top: Gerald Cubitt/NHPA/Photoshot/Newscom; 5 bottom: Martin
Harvey/Alamy Images; 7: Wolfgang Kaehler/Getty Images; 8: Nick
Garbutt/Minden Pictures; 11: Gerald Cubitt/NHPA/Photoshot/Newscom;
12: Mint Images-Frans Lanting/Getty Images; 15: Suzi Eszterhas/Minden
Pictures; 16: Inaki Relanzon/Minden Pictures; 19: Paul Souders/Getty
Images; 20: Minden Pictures/Superstock, Inc.; 23: Duncan Usher/Alamy
Images; 24: Kevin Schafer/Alamy Images; 27: Adam Seward/Alamy Images;
28: Dennis van de Water/Shutterstock, Inc.; 31: Nick
Garbutt/NHPA/Photoshot/Newscom; 32: Minden Pictures/Superstock, Inc.;
35: Juniors Bildarchiv GmbH/Alamy Images; 36: Martin Harvey/Alamy
Images; 39: Pete Oxford/Minden Pictures; 40: Philip Dumas/Getty Images;
44-45 background: Genarosilva/Dreamstime; 46: Andriy Dykun/Dreamstime.

Map by Bob Italiano.

Library of Congress Cataloging-in-Publication Data
Names: Gregory, Josh, author.
Title: Lemurs / by Josh Gregory.
Other titles: Nature's children (New York, N.Y.)
Description: New York, NY : Children's Press, an imprint of Scholastic Inc.,
   [2017] | Series: Nature's children | Includes bibliographical references
   and index.
Identifiers: LCCN 2015043582| ISBN 9780531230312 (library binding)
| ISBN 9780531219379 (pbk.)
Subjects: LCSH: Lemurs—Juvenile literature. | Lemurs—Behavior—Juvenile
   literature.
Classification: LCC QL737.P95 G74 2017 | DDC 599.8/3—dc23
LC record available at http://lccn.loc.gov/2015043582

Printed in China 62
SCHOLASTIC, CHILDREN'S PRESS, and associated logos are trademarks
and/or registered trademarks of Scholastic Inc.

1 2 3 4 5 6 7 8 9 10 R 26 25 24 23 22 21 20 19 18 17

Lemurs

Class	Mammalia
Order	Primates
Family	Cheirogaleidae (dwarf and mouse lemurs), Daubentoniidae (aye-aye), Indriidae (indri, sifakas), Lemuridae (lemurs, bamboo lemurs), Lepilemuridae (sportive lemurs)
Genera	Around 15 genera
Species	Around 100 species
World distribution	Madagascar and the Comoro Islands
Habitats	Forests, wetlands, and mountains
Distinctive physical characteristics	Most have long, slender bodies and limbs; most also have long bushy tails; large eyes; fur colored in shades of black, brown, white, and red, with various markings and patterns; padded hands and feet for jumping and climbing; five digits on each hand and foot, with thumbs for grasping objects
Habits	Usually spends most of its time in trees; most species live together in family groups; others form monogamous pairs or live solitary lives; mates during a short breeding season each year; usually produces a single offspring at a time
Diet	Diets vary greatly from species to species; common foods include fruit, plants, and insects

Contents

CHAPTER 1

Leaping through the Treetops

It is a warm, sunny day in the dense, green forests of Madagascar. There is activity all around. Among the animals out and about in this beautiful environment are several furry creatures. They hop across the ground on all fours. Held high in the air, their long tails are striped in black and white. They are ring-tailed lemurs.

The lemurs expertly hop from the ground to a nearby tree trunk and climb up. One by one, they clamber out onto one of the tree's long, narrow branches. As the first lemur reaches the end of the branch, it uses its strong back legs to leap into the air. The lemur lands on the branch of another tree several feet away and keeps moving forward. It seems like a once-in-a-lifetime leap, but the other lemurs in the group have no trouble following their friend. These amazing acrobatics are just an everyday part of life for lemurs.

A Verreaux's sifaka leaps between trees.

A Lemur's Looks

There are roughly 100 different kinds of lemurs living today. The ring-tailed lemur is one of the best-known species. Aside from the "true lemurs" such as this one, animals such as indris, avahis, sifakas, and aye-ayes are all considered lemurs.

Though each lemur species is unique, they all share some basic characteristics. These animals tend to have long, slender bodies. Their arms and legs are also very long. This shape makes them look somewhat like monkeys. Most lemurs also have long, bushy tails. Some species' tails, however, are short and stubby.

A lemur's fur is soft and fuzzy. It is usually colored in shades of black, brown, white, and red. Many species have stripes, spots, and other patterns in their fur.

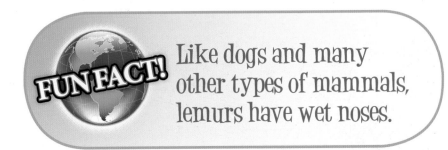

FUN FACT! Like dogs and many other types of mammals, lemurs have wet noses.

Aye-ayes have extra-long middle fingers that they use to find and grab insects.

Lemurs Large and Small

Lemurs vary greatly in size from species to species. The smallest is the Madame Berthe's mouse lemur. Named for its mouselike appearance, it measures just 3.5 to 4 inches (9 to 10 centimeters) from the tip of its nose to the base of its tail. Its tail is another 5 inches (13 cm) or so long. This tiny lemur weighs just 1 ounce (28 grams). In addition to being the smallest lemur species, it is also the smallest primate living today.

The largest lemur is the indri. Its body is around 24 to 35 inches (61 to 89 cm) long. Unlike the mouse lemur, it has only a short stub of a tail. A fully grown indri weighs between 15.5 and 22 pounds (7 and 10 kilograms). That is around 250 to 350 times the weight of a Madame Berthe's mouse lemur!

Adult male
6 ft. (1.8 m)

Indri body
35 in. (89 cm) long

Madame Berthe's
mouse lemur body
3.5 in. (9 cm) long

The Madame Berthe's mouse lemur was
first recognized as a species in 2000.

An Island Home

Though there are many different kinds of lemurs, all of these animals live within a fairly small area. Wild lemurs are found only on the island of Madagascar and the nearby Comoro Islands. Madagascar is located about 250 miles (402 kilometers) from the east coast of Africa. The Comoro Islands are just to the northwest of Madagascar.

Madagascar and its nearby islands are a unique area. A large number of the animals and plants that live there are not found anywhere else on Earth. Madagascar is completely different from Africa, despite being located so close to it. It is a land of thick forests, rocky mountains, swampy wetlands, and sandy beaches. Lemurs live throughout the island in all of these different habitats. Each species has special traits and skills to help it survive in its native environment.

Many lemurs live among stone "towers," carved by water into sharp peaks over time, in Madagascar's Tsingy de Bemaraha Strict Nature Reserve.

CHAPTER 2

Day to Day

Like many wild animals, lemurs spend much of their time searching for and eating food. Because there are so many different types of lemurs living in different habitats, diets vary quite a bit from species to species. Most of the smaller lemurs have a diet consisting mainly of fruit and insects. Bigger lemurs don't usually eat insects. Instead, they tend to eat a wider variety of plant parts. Leaves, flowers, sap, and bark might all be on the menu for one of these primates. Not all large lemurs are vegetarians, though. Some species also hunt small animals such as birds. Eggs are a common meal as well.

Some lemurs have very specific diets. For example, bamboo lemurs live in a part of Madagascar where bamboo is especially common. As a result, the plant makes up almost all of their diet. Another species, the reed lemur, lives in a swampy area where reed plants grow. These reeds are this lemur's main food source.

A ring-tailed lemur takes a bite from a flower.

Alert and Aware

To survive in the wild habitats of Madagascar, lemurs must be aware of their surroundings at all times. Aside from keeping an eye out for food, they also have to avoid dangerous **predators**. Snakes can pop out of hiding spots to snatch an unsuspecting lemur. Birds of prey can attack from above. The fossa, a catlike animal found only in Madagascar, can jump and climb through the treetops to chase down lemurs.

Lemurs rely on their sharp senses to detect and avoid threats. In general, smell is a lemur's most important sense. A lemur can pick up the scent of predators, other lemurs, and food from far away. Vision is also very important. Lemurs cannot see things in sharp detail. However, they can see very well in the dark. This is especially helpful for the many **nocturnal** lemur species. Even lemurs that are active mostly during the day use this night vision. They rely on it when keeping a lookout during evenings and early mornings.

A Sahamalaza sportive lemur peeks out from its hiding place in a hollow tree.

Leaping Lemurs

All lemurs spend at least part of their time in trees. Some species travel on the ground frequently, but there are many that hardly ever leave the treetops at all. As a result, climbing and jumping play major roles in the way lemurs travel from place to place.

Lemurs usually move on all four limbs. They have **opposable** thumbs on their hands and feet. This means each limb can grab things the same way a human hand does. Special pads on their hands and feet allow lemurs to grip trees without slipping or injuring themselves. This helps them shimmy up the sides of trees and run across limbs. A lemur's long tail helps it stay balanced as it moves across narrow branches. Many lemur species also have especially long and powerful back legs. This gives them the strength they need to make long leaps between trees that are far apart.

Lemurs sometimes hang upside down by gripping a branch with their back feet.

Keeping It Clean

Because they spend so much time hopping along the ground and speeding through trees, it is easy for lemurs to become dirty. Bits of plants get stuck in their fur. Bugs climb onto them. They become muddy or wet. However, lemurs never stay messy for long. When they are not busy eating or sleeping, they like to groom themselves or each other.

On the second toe of each foot of a lemur is a tool called a toilet claw. This special claw is longer than the others. It is perfect for picking through another lemur's fur in search of bugs or other things that don't belong there. Lemurs also use their lower front teeth to comb through each other's fur. These teeth are long and narrow with small gaps between them. They look very much like the teeth of the combs that humans use.

A baby lemur might receive a bath from any lemur in its troop—not just its mom!

CHAPTER 3

A Lemur's Life

Most lemur species are very social. They live together in family groups called troops. The size of these groups varies from species to species. Some troops might only have four or five members, while others might contain as many as 30 lemurs. Each troop has a dominant female. She leads the other members from place to place in search of food and shelter. The members of a troop travel together and help one another watch for danger. They also groom and play with one another. Adult members of the group all **mate** around the same time each year.

Some lemurs that live in smaller groups include dwarf lemurs. This species forms **monogamous** couples. These pairs live and travel together throughout their lives. Other species are fairly **solitary**. They do not spend a lot of time with other lemurs unless it is time for them to mate.

Ring-tailed lemurs have some of the largest troops among lemur species.

Something to Say

Lemurs have many ways to communicate with fellow troop members, rivals, and potential mates. Different species make different kinds of noises. Some use low grunting sounds, while others make high-pitched chirps. These noises can warn other troop members that a predator is near or communicate other important information.

Smell also plays a major role in lemur communication. Lemurs spread smells using their urine as well as special scent glands. For example, ring-tailed lemurs have scent glands on their wrists. Special fingernail-like body parts called spurs are located near these glands. The spurs are covered in the glands' scent. Male troop members scratch their spurs against trees to leave scent behind to mark their territory. When other troops smell it, they know to stay away.

Some lemur calls are loud and can be heard from a long distance away.

Mating Season

Lemurs also rely on their scent glands to fend off rivals during mating season. When male ring-tailed lemurs are competing for the attention of a female, they often have "stink fights." First, they rub their tails on their wrists to transfer scent from their glands. Then they face off and wave their tails in each other's faces. Eventually, one of the lemurs will give up.

Mating season arrives once every year for lemurs. The exact time is different for each species, but it is usually very short. Some species mate only on a single day each year.

A lemur mother is ready to give birth between two and five months after mating, depending on the species. In most cases, only a single baby is born at a time. However, some species are able to have up to six babies each time they mate.

A male ring-tailed lemur rubs his tail against scent glands on his wrist.

The Road to Adulthood

Baby lemurs have the same general appearance as their parents, though they are much smaller. For the first several weeks of their life, most species spend almost all of their time holding tight to their mother's belly. They go everywhere she goes, and they feed by drinking milk she produces. Once it gets a little bigger, a baby lemur can ride on its mother's back. It does this more and more until it no longer spends any time on her stomach. This happens when the lemur is around three to four weeks old.

At about this age, the baby lemur starts to eat solid food along with its mother's milk. As it grows older, the young lemur eventually stops drinking milk completely. It also starts to move around on its own. By the time it is around five to six months old, the lemur can survive without its mother's help.

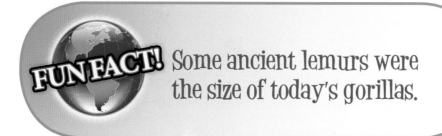

FUN FACT! Some ancient lemurs were the size of today's gorillas.

Two young red-fronted brown lemurs cling to their mother.

CHAPTER 4

Ancestors and Relatives

Lemurs have been living in Madagascar for tens of millions of years. Scientists believe their ancestors traveled to Madagascar from Africa around 60 million years ago. They probably did this by accident, floating away on huge chunks of plant material. Later, lemurs spread to the nearby Comoro Islands, most likely brought by humans.

Lemur ancestors were probably a lot like the lemurs living today. However, they were not the exact same animals. Over time, lemurs in different parts of Madagascar changed to meet the demands of their particular habitats. Groups became more and more different from one another, resulting in the species living today.

To study the history of lemurs and their ancestors, scientists dig up fossils of these ancient species. These remains help experts figure out where different species lived, when they first appeared or died out, and how they changed over time.

Ancient lemurs left behind many traces in the forms of bones and other fossils.

Lemurs and Lorisiformes

The closest living relatives of today's lemurs are a group of animals known as Lorisiformes. These animals look and behave much like lemurs do. However, they do not live in Madagascar or the Comoro Islands. Lorisiformes called lorises are found in many parts of southern and Southeast Asia. Unlike many lemurs, lorises have very short, stubby tails. They also have very big eyes ringed with darkly colored fur. This gives their faces a distinctive appearance.

The potto is a Lorisiforme that lives in the rain forests of Africa. It often eats poisonous or bad-tasting insects and other bugs that most animals won't go near. This means there is always plenty for pottos to eat.

Like pottos, Lorisiformes called bush babies are also found in Africa. They have large eyes like lorises and larger ears than lemurs. In addition to eating fruit and insects, they often dig holes in trees to get at the sticky gum inside.

Lorises are nocturnal. Their large eyes help them see at night.

Primate Cousins

Besides lemurs and their close relatives, there are many other primates living today. These animals include monkeys, apes, and even humans. Though these animals are not closely related to lemurs, they share common ancestors. As lemurs appeared in and near Madagascar, these other primates developed elsewhere around the world.

While they might not look a lot alike, lemurs and other primates have many things in common. For example, humans, apes, and many monkeys have opposable thumbs, just as lemurs do. Very few other animals share this characteristic. Like lemurs, many monkeys have long tails and limbs. They also spend a lot of time in trees and are good at climbing and jumping.

FUN FACT! There are more than 300 primate species living today.

Just like many other primates, chimpanzees spend much of their time in trees.

CHAPTER 5

Living with Lemurs

For a very long time, ancient lemurs and other animals lived on Madagascar without ever meeting humans. They faced few natural threats, and they thrived on their island home. It wasn't until about 2,000 years ago that people came to Madagascar for the first time. These people and their descendants brought great changes to the island. Unfortunately, these changes have mostly had negative effects on lemurs. Scientists estimate that at least 16 lemur species have gone extinct since humans first founded settlements in Madagascar. Many fascinating, unique animals are gone forever.

This happened in part because people took over wild habitats to build homes, farms, and other structures. Also, people hunted lemurs as a source of food. They were not worried about keeping lemur species from dying out. They were only concerned about getting enough to eat.

As the human population on Madagascar grows, humans and lemurs share more space.

A Threat to Survival

Today, people are more aware of the need to protect animal species from extinction. However, human actions still cause a great deal of harm to lemurs and other wild animals. Many lemur species are listed as endangered or threatened. In fact, lemurs as a whole are considered one of the most endangered animal groups in the world. Some experts believe lemurs could disappear from Madagascar completely within decades if nothing is done to save them.

Habitat destruction is the biggest threat facing lemurs today. Of all the wildland once occupied by lemurs, only 20 percent remains unspoiled today. People continue to cut down trees in Madagascar to clear space or to harvest wood. Mining also damages the land and reduces the amount of space where lemurs can live. Additionally, some people in rural areas of the country continue to hunt lemurs to eat. They are often too poor to afford other food.

Mines in Madagascar have resulted in deforestation and unhealthy habitats.

Protecting Lemurs

Many conservation groups are doing their best to protect lemurs from extinction. However, this is no easy task. The government of Madagascar does not have enough money to spend on protecting wild animals. There are laws to protect lemurs and their habitats, but there are no law enforcement officers, fences, or other obstacles to keep hunters away.

Conservation groups in Madagascar hope that tourists will bring money into the country to help protect lemurs. Another source of money could be foreign investors who want to help. Either way, the fight to save lemurs will be difficult. The people of Madagascar will need a better understanding of how and why these endangered animals should be protected. The government of Madagascar will need to fight against illegal mining and logging operations that destroy forests. It will be a long road, but every step in the right direction could help make it easier for lemurs to survive.

People at tree nurseries grow and care for new trees in the forests of Madagascar.

Words to Know

ancestors (AN-ses-turz) — ancient animal species that are related to modern species

conservation (kahn-sur-VAY-shuhn) — the protection of valuable things, especially forests, wildlife, natural resources, or artistic or historic objects

endangered (en-DAYN-jurd) — at risk of becoming extinct, usually because of human activity

extinct (ik-STINGKT) — no longer found alive

fossils (FAH-suhlz) — the hardened remains of prehistoric plants and animals

glands (GLANDZ) — organs in the body that produce or release natural chemicals

groom (GROOM) — to brush and clean

habitats (HAB-uh-tats) — places where an animal or a plant is usually found

mate (MAYT) — to join together to produce babies

monogamous (mah-NAH-guh-mus) — the practice of having a single mate during a lifetime

nocturnal (nahk-TUR-nuhl) — active at night

opposable (uh-POHZ-uh-buhl) — able to be placed against one or more of the remaining fingers or toes of a hand or foot

predators (PREH-duh-turz) — animals that live by hunting other animals for food

primate (PRYE-mate) — any member of the group of mammals that includes monkeys, apes, and humans

solitary (SAH-lih-ter-ee) — preferring to live alone

species (SPEE-sheez) — one of the groups into which animals and plants of the same genus are divided

territory (TER-uh-tor-ee) — an area of land claimed by a given individual or group

threatened (THRET-uhnd) — at risk of becoming endangered

Habitat Map

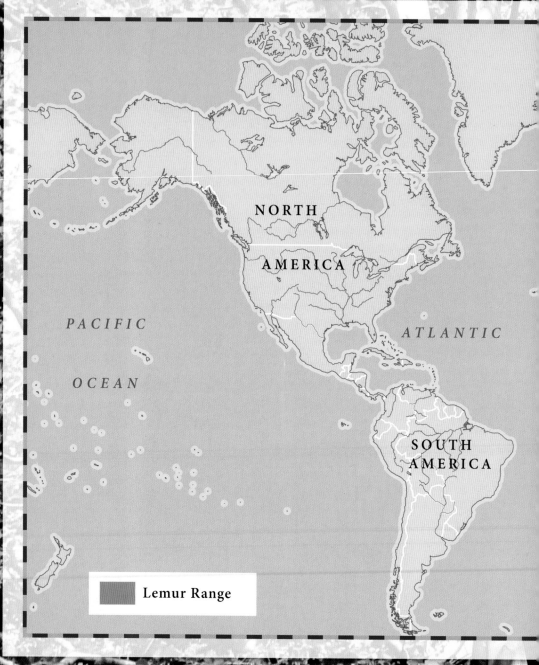

NORTH

AMERICA

PACIFIC

OCEAN

ATLANTIC

SOUTH
AMERICA

Lemur Range

ARCTIC OCEAN

EUROPE

ASIA

AFRICA

PACIFIC OCEAN

INDIAN OCEAN

OCEAN

Madagascar

Comoro Islands

AUSTRALIA

Find Out More

Book

Schuetz, Kari. *Lemurs.* Minneapolis: Bellwether Media, 2013.

Visit this Scholastic Web site for more information on lemurs:
www.factsfornow.scholastic.com
Enter the keyword **Lemurs**

Index

Page numbers in *italics* indicate a photograph or map.

About the Author

Josh Gregory is the author of more than 90 books for kids. He has written about everything from animals to technology to history. A graduate of the University of Missouri-Columbia, he currently lives in Portland, Oregon.